DISCOVERING THE UNITED STATES

North Carolina

BY DONNA B. McKINNEY

An Imprint of Abdo Publishing
abdobooks.com

abdobooks.com

Printed in China.
052024
092024

Cover Photo: Margaret Wiktor/Shutterstock Images
Interior Photos: Bettmann/Getty Images, 4–5; iStockphoto, 6; Stephen B. Goodwin/Shutterstock Images, 7; Kyle J. Little/Shutterstock Images, 9; Margaret Wiktor/Shutterstock Images, 10; John Wollwerth/Alamy, 12–13; Bonnie Taylor Barry/Shutterstock Images, 14 (top left); Brian Lasenby/Shutterstock Images, 14 (top right); Jorge Salcedo/Shutterstock Images, 14 (bottom left); Shutterstock Images, 14 (bottom right), 25, 26; Josh Lavallee/National Hockey League/Getty Images, 17; B. Christopher/Alamy, 18; Sean Pavone/Shutterstock Images, 20–21, 29 (bottom right); D. Guest Smith/Alamy, 22; Red Line Editorial, 28 (top), 29 (top); Jay Yuan/Shutterstock Images, 28 (bottom); Margaret Wiktor/Shutterstock Images, 29 (bottom left)

Editor: Marley Richmond
Series Designer: Katharine Hale

Library of Congress Control Number: 2023949336

Publisher's Cataloging-in-Publication Data

Names: McKinney, Donna B., author.
Title: North Carolina / by Donna B. McKinney
Description: Minneapolis, Minnesota: Abdo Publishing, 2025 | Series: Discovering the United States | Includes online resources and index.
Identifiers: ISBN 9781098294038 (lib. bdg.) | ISBN 9798384913306 (ebook)
Subjects: LCSH: U.S. states--Juvenile literature. | North Carolina--History--Juvenile literature. | Southeastern States--Juvenile literature. | Physical geography--United States--Juvenile literature.
Classification: DDC 973--dc23

All population data taken from:
"Estimates of Population by Sex, Race, and Hispanic Origin: April 1, 2020 to July 1, 2022." *US Census Bureau, Population Division,* June 2023, census.gov.

CONTENTS

Wilbur Wright watches as his brother Orville flies their plane.

CHAPTER 1

Wright Brothers' Flight

In 1903, Orville and Wilbur Wright got ready to fly their airplane. They stood on a sandy beach in North Carolina. The brothers studied flight and **gliders**. They built a plane from wood and fabric. Now they needed a place to test their plane.

North Carolina has used the same flag since March 9, 1885. This flag is based on a version used during the American Civil War (1861–1865).

The brothers chose a beach with steady wind in Kitty Hawk, North Carolina. The ocean breeze and the soft sandy beaches in Kitty Hawk were perfect. On December 17, 1903,

The Wright Brothers' first flight was on a beach in Kitty Hawk. Today, the area still has the perfect wind for flying.

the brothers' flight made history. It was the first successful flight of a motor-powered airplane.

That first flight lasted 12 seconds. North Carolina still celebrates the Wright brothers. The state's license plates say, "First in Flight."

North Carolina Geography

North Carolina is in the South region of the United States. It sits on the Atlantic coast. Virginia is to the north. South Carolina and Georgia are to the south. Tennessee is to the west.

The state's weather varies. Snow falls in winter. Summers are hot and **humid**. The state

A Living Sand Dune

The tallest sand dune on the US East Coast is in Jockey's Ridge State Park on North Carolina's **barrier islands**. These islands are called the Outer Banks. Ocean winds are always moving the sands back and forth. The winds change the dune's shape. So this sand dune is sometimes called the Living Dune.

North Carolina's barrier islands help protect the mainland from ocean storms.

averages 44 inches (112 cm) of rain each year. It gets about 5 inches (13 cm) of snow.

North Carolina has different geographic regions. The coastal plain is near the ocean. There are **marshes** in this area. Along the coast, there are also **barrier islands**.

The Blue Ridge Mountains run through western North Carolina.

The center of the state is called the piedmont. The piedmont is a **plateau**. The western part of the state is the mountain region. The Eastern Continental Divide is in the mountains. This divide separates rivers flowing east and west. Rivers east of the divide flow to the Atlantic Ocean. Rivers west of the divide flow toward the Gulf of Mexico.

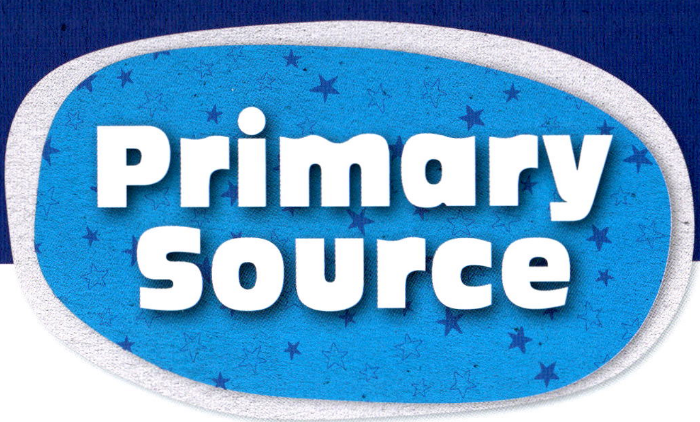

Wilbur Wright described Kitty Hawk, North Carolina. He said:

> In October my brother and myself spent a vacation of several weeks at Kitty Hawk, North Carolina, experimenting with a soaring machine. . . . It is the ideal place for gliding experiments except for its **inaccessibility**.

Source: "Commemorating the Wright Brothers at Kitty Hawk." *National Park Service*, n.d., nps.gov. Accessed 26 Sept. 2023.

Comparing Texts

Think about the quote. Does it support facts in this chapter? Or does it give a different view? Explain how in a few sentences.

Some Cherokee people still practice traditional arts such as beadwork.

The People of North Carolina

The first people to live on the land now called North Carolina arrived more than 10,000 years ago. American Indians in this area hunted for food. Over time, they began to raise crops and create art. They built towns and formed governments.

North Carolina Facts

DATE OF STATEHOOD
November 21, 1789

CAPITAL
Raleigh

POPULATION
10,698,973

AREA
53,819 square miles
(139,391 sq km)

STATE BIRD

Northern cardinal

STATE TREE

Pine

STATE FLOWER

Dogwood

STATE SHELL

Scotch bonnet

Each US state has a different population, size, and capital city. States also have state symbols.

American Indians are still in the state today. The federal government officially recognizes one American Indian nation in North Carolina. It is the Eastern Band of Cherokee Indians.

Europeans settled along the Pamlico River in the 1690s. **Settlers** continued to spread across the area. North Carolina became a state almost 100 years later in 1789.

People and Work

More than 10 million people now live in North Carolina. In the state, more than 60 percent of people are white. About 20 percent are Black. Ten percent are Hispanic or Latino. About 3 percent are Asian, and 1 percent are American Indian.

The state's main industries range from banking to hog farming. Many people have jobs making fabric, furniture, and more. Some North Carolinians work in Research Triangle Park.

This park is near the cities of Raleigh and Durham. It is home to hundreds of technology companies. Government groups and universities also operate in Research Triangle Park.

Sports and Food

North Carolinians love sports. Many people cheer on the Carolina Hurricanes in ice hockey.

All That Jazz

North Carolina has been home to many famous jazz musicians. Jazz combines African and European music styles. One famous jazz musician from North Carolina was John Coltrane. He was inspired by other jazz musicians during his childhood in the state. He went on to release many famous albums.

Fans watch the Carolina Hurricanes at PNC Arena in Raleigh, North Carolina.

The first Krispy Kreme donut shop opened in Winston-Salem, North Carolina, in 1937.

Fans also support the Carolina Panthers in professional football. North Carolina is known for college basketball and NASCAR racing too.

North Carolina is home to some famous foods and drinks. Pepsi-Cola and Cheerwine are two popular soft drinks invented in the state. Krispy Kreme donuts were also invented in North Carolina. Pork barbecue has been a popular food across the state since the 1800s. The fried chicken restaurant Bojangles started in the state as well.

Explore Online

Look at the website below. What more do you learn about the history and people of North Carolina?

North Carolina

abdocorelibrary.com/discovering-north-carolina

The main area of Charlotte, North Carolina, is known as Uptown Charlotte.

Places in North Carolina

Charlotte is the largest city in North Carolina. It is near the Catawba River. The NASCAR Hall of Fame is in Charlotte. The US National Whitewater Center is also in the city. There, athletes train in sports such as white water rafting.

People paddle canoes and kayaks through the Dismal Swamp Canal.

Raleigh is the second-largest city in the state. It is the state capital. Raleigh is in the center of North Carolina. There are three major museums in Raleigh. North Carolina's Museum of Art is there. So is its Museum of History. The Museum of Natural Sciences is the largest natural history museum in the southeastern United States.

Parks

North Carolina has 41 state parks. The parks are all different. Dismal Swamp State Park is part of the largest swamp in the eastern United States. Mount Mitchell State Park has the highest point east of the Mississippi River. Mount Mitchell is part of the Appalachian Mountains.

The Cape Hatteras Lighthouse sits on US parklands near the coast. The lighthouse was completed in 1870 to guide sailors to safety. The dangerous ocean waters in the area were called the Graveyard of the Atlantic.

Places to Visit

The Biltmore Estate in Asheville is called America's Largest Home. The 250-room castle

Hike across North Carolina

The Mountains-to-Sea State Trail stretches from North Carolina's western border in the mountains to the Atlantic Coast. Parts of the long hiking trail are still being built. The trail will be 1,400 miles (2,250 km) long when finished.

It took six years to build the Biltmore Estate.

sits on 8,000 acres (3,320 ha) of land. It is open for visitors to tour. The wealthy Vanderbilt family started to build the estate in 1889.

The Battleship North Carolina is a floating museum. It is docked in Wilmington. The ship is a World War II (1939–1945) memorial. It honors those who died fighting in the war. Guests can tour the ship and see where the sailors worked and lived.

Jennette's Pier is 1,000 feet (305 m) long.

Jennette's Pier is home to one of the North Carolina Aquariums. It is also a fishing pier. People can catch black drum, bluefish, croaker, flounder, and sea trout from the ocean. The Pier is on the Outer Banks. It has exhibits where guests can learn about ocean life along the coast.

From the mountains to the ocean, North Carolina is a great place to visit or live. People can watch NASCAR racing and eat any of the state's food inventions. They can explore state parks or visit great museums. There is something for everyone there.

Further Evidence

Look at the website below. Does it give any new evidence to support Chapter Three?

Appalachians

abdocorelibrary.com/discovering-north-carolina

State Map

KEY

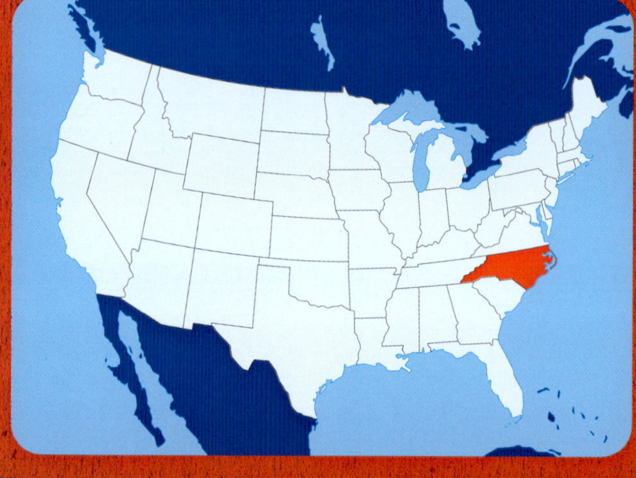

Cape Hatteras Lighthouse

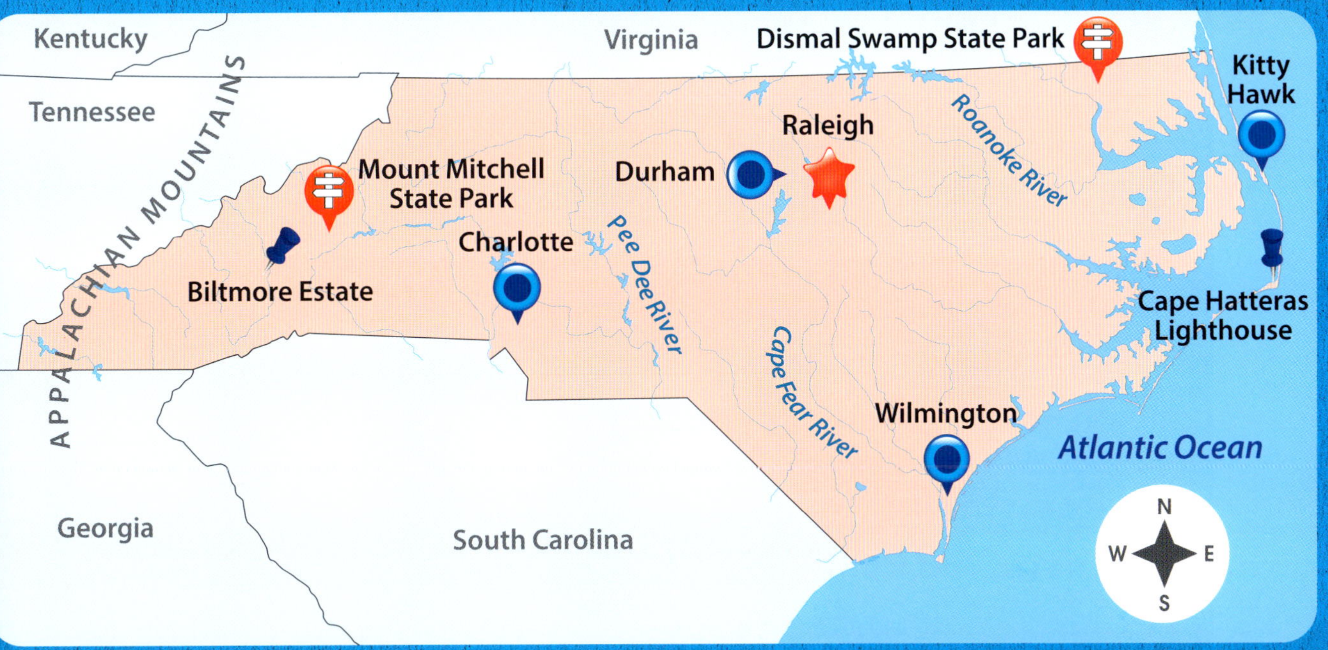

Mount Mitchell State Park

Wilmington

Glossary

barrier islands
narrow strips of sand that form offshore islands

gliders
light airplanes that fly without using an engine

humid
describing air that has a lot of moisture

inaccessibility
difficulty of reaching or accessing

marshes
areas of soft wet land

plateau
an area of land that is high and flat

settlers
people who moved to a new area

Online Resources

To learn more about North Carolina, visit our free resource websites below.

Visit **abdocorelibrary.com** or scan this QR code for free Common Core resources for teachers and students, including vetted activities, multimedia, and booklinks, for deeper subject comprehension.

Visit **abdobooklinks.com** or scan this QR code for free additional online weblinks for further learning. These links are routinely monitored and updated to provide the most current information available.

Learn More

Murray, Julie. *North Carolina.* Abdo, 2020.

Whipple, Annette. *The Story of the Wright Brothers.* Rockridge, 2020.

Index

About the Author

Donna B. McKinney is the author of more than 20 nonfiction books for young people on topics including science, technology, history, sports, and current events. McKinney spent many years writing about science and technology topics at the US Naval Research Laboratory in Washington, DC. She has a BA in English from Campbell University and an MA in English from George Mason University. She lives in North Carolina.